Toxic Connections:

Freeing Your Demons

Moonsoulchild

Toxic Connections: Freeing Your Demons

Toxic Connections: Freeing Your Demons

Sara Sheehan 2021 Copyright

All Rights Reserved

ISBN: 9798713496951

The Feelings & Healing Collection:

Finding Self: Journey to Self-Love
Healthy Connections: Guide on Relationships
Grief: Process of Healing

Broken: For the Ones Picking Up the Pieces
Discovering: For the Soul Searchers
Twin Souls: For the Lovers

Toxic Connections: Freeing Your Demons
Healing: The Journey of Growth
Soulmates: Not All Are in the Form of Lovers
Insecurities: Empowering Self

Freeing Your Demons

    A toxic connection is quite common in every relationship, even within yourself. We encounter toxicity every day, whether it's within ourselves or within someone we love. It's not often our loved ones or we take accountability for our toxic traits, as we're blinded by them or the love we have for someone; it's hard to see through that love. It's evident love is the main thing that keeps us in a toxic connection, as we convinced ourselves to believe love is the answer, at all costs, even when it cost your mental and physical wellbeing. You find yourself draining everything you must give. You find yourself lacking the sensibility to grow because you're finding it hard to leave the ones holding you back. This book is all about realizing your toxic traits and letting go of everyone who's toxic to your being. To set free every demon you're holding onto, it's time to let go.

Toxic Connections: Freeing Your Demons

Don't forget to **cut that toxic person off** today.

Toxic Connections: Freeing Your Demons

What's a "Toxic Relationship"?

1. *Putting all your time, energy, and attention into someone while neglecting yourself.* Make sure they're good before checking on you. Completely forget you exist trying to make/keep them happy.

I thought caring more about my loved ones was healthy until I realized it wasn't when I cared more about them than I did about myself. I stopped things I loved to fit into their lifestyle. I changed parts of myself to be what they needed. Their healing journey became top on my priority list until I realized I wasn't anyone's savior.

2. *Being a savior.*
No one truly needs you to save them. They need you to love them and be there for them. Letting someone be dependent on you will cause them to

> take advantage of all you have to give.
> It will cost you exhausting yourself. You
> will end up more lost than you were,
> causing you to forget your worth along
> the way.

I constantly adapted to ones who needed saving and were desperate for healing. I attracted the broken because I felt so broken. I knew my love was enough. I knew my kind of soul would help anyone heal. Instead, they used my heart as a weapon against me. They used me for their gain and left me once they felt whole.

3. *Any form of abuse.*
   It may not be recognized; first, you may become blinded by "love." No form of abuse is okay. If someone thinks they have the power to control your mind, body, and life, that's not something you should overlook. Don't stay.

I've been mentally, emotionally, and physically abused. I experienced rape my first time having sex. I didn't think of it like that because I was blinded by the love I had for him. The

Toxic Connections: Freeing Your Demons

discomfort I feel from the memories and experiences that trigger the PTSD from the one moment that lead to many uncomfortable moments with that one person lead to troubles in my days after him.

All abuse cuts deep; neither is worse than the other. I've been with someone who completely shut me out while he was mad, we lived together, and I was nonexistent. When he was over it, it was never brought up; it was never communicated. I was left wondering. I was left with a constant emotional build-up that turned to rage and a lot of pain.

4. *Always blaming yourself.*
   Not giving yourself the proper credit. When something goes wrong, you always blame yourself. You try to fix something you didn't destruct. You do everything in your power to prevent a fight. You do everything to keep them happy. This will dig you deeper into thinking you're the problem.

The many times I was shut out, I blamed myself. Why couldn't I help? Why did I let it get this far? Am I not enough? I blamed myself when it was his insecurities that were the problem. It got so far to the point I thought something was wrong with me. It was easy to blame myself instead of seeing him as the problem, the love I had for him blinded me to the problem between us for so long.

5. *No life.*
    Shutting out your passions, dreams, and everything you love. Not being able to recognize yourself. If you find yourself walking away from who you are and everything you love, run. If you find yourself forgetting everything that once brought you happiness while relying on just that one person for it, run.

I didn't realize I was secluded; it was the first time I was in a real relationship. I thought I was enjoying it. I gave up my writing. I lost my direction in life. I stopped seeing my family as much as I did. I found myself always at their need; the codependency on their end was slowly killing me.

Toxic Connections: Freeing Your Demons

6. *Making excuses for your toxic relationship.*
   Don't discredit what's in front of you; open your eyes. Love isn't all there is to life. Love is a blessing, but if you need to belittle yourself, lose yourself, and give up everything for it, it's not it.

There were many times I would question my connections. There were many times I wanted to speak up, but I was afraid to lose everything I once worked so hard to get. I was blinded by what I thought love was. I was blinded by the idea I made up for someone I latched myself to believe. I was blinded by the toxicity.

7. *Take accountability.*
   Take part in your toxic traits. Understand you may have picked up some bad behavior along the way. If you've struggled with previous relationship traits, acknowledge them and heal from them before you let anyone close to loving you.

Toxic Connections: Freeing Your Demons

My toxic traits were loving and giving too much when they didn't deserve it. Ghosting without giving them closure. It was neglecting myself, not giving myself true love. It was selfish to myself try to save, heal, and make someone love me when I couldn't even love myself.

Being in toxic connections, I realized I played my part in being the problem. I let others get so close to me; I let them control me. The walls I built never had the proper foundation. I fantasized about love so much, I gave in every time someone came close. I accepted that. I've healed because of it.

Relationships, friendships, family. They all can be toxic. They don't need to be kept around if it's not healthy for your soul. It's okay to walk away from someone you thought you loved. People change, and sometimes for the worst, you need to accept that.

One of the most significant troubles people face is not opening their eyes sooner because of "love." Let me tell you, love isn't loving if you're the only one putting yourself out there. If you're being treated less than you're worth. It's a sign you deserve to set yourself free.

Toxic Connections: Freeing Your Demons

No more excuses.

No more trying to heal them.

No more trying to understand their brokenness.

No more wasting time.

It's time to open your eyes and see the reality in front of you before it's too late. I know it hurts being an empath, but it's time to save yourself.

Toxic Connections: Freeing Your Demons

Tell me about a toxic relationship you were in:

_____

_____

_____

_____

_____

_____

_____

_____

_____

_____

_____

_____

_____

Toxic Connections: Freeing Your Demons

Tell me when you were toxic to yourself:

_____
_____
_____
_____
_____
_____
_____
_____
_____
_____
_____
_____
_____

In the past, what were your toxic traits?

Toxic Connections: Freeing Your Demons

Cut off that toxic person in your life today.

Open your eyes.

Let them go.

If you're not being respected, the love you're giving but isn't being reciprocated, it's not worth being treated wrong.

Love isn't enough to stay.

Toxic Connections: Freeing Your Demons

Don't keep company who drain you with their toxic aura. You don't need that type of negativity surrounding your heart.

Toxic Connections: Freeing Your Demons

Love can be blinding when it comes to years of knowing and growing with someone. We condition ourselves to believe love overpowers everything, forgetting people can change and creating toxic behavior. Sometimes, *we confuse that with love.*

Toxic Connections: Freeing Your Demons

Know the difference between love, and love that only lives within you. *The love that you hold sometimes can be toxic to yourself* because the love isn't reciprocated. **A toxic love can blind** you from ever seeing what real love is like.

Toxic Connections: Freeing Your Demons

You can't always blame others
For the way they treat you,
When *you're the one allowing* them to.

Maybe you hold some toxic traits too.

If you can't ever admit to being wrong
And holding toxic traits from the past,
Letting them shape you,
How are you supposed to grow?

I'm mature enough to admit *I held some toxic traits too*, and how I let myself be consumed by you. I'm mature enough to admit I wasn't perfect; **I know I brought pain too**.

Toxic Connections: Freeing Your Demons

I became toxic to myself, keeping myself away from growing in the direction without the ones I loved, but the continued signs showed they weren't for me. *Having a big heart almost broke me*, but in the end, **it only built me**. I couldn't have found the version of me without the pain.

Toxic Connections: Freeing Your Demons

Normalize taking accountability
for your toxic traits
before *you hold anyone accountable for theirs*.

Toxic Connections: Freeing Your Demons

We are all toxic to someone because we forced love when the chapter was already written when the book was already closed. Our intentions were pure, but the person and situation weren't right. **We became toxic by chasing everything we wished to feel**.

**Tell me,
How did you part ways with your toxic traits?**

_____
_____
_____
_____
_____
_____
_____
_____
_____
_____
_____
_____
_____
_____

Toxic Connections: Freeing Your Demons

My ex had toxic traits; he'd also tell you I was toxic too. I can't correct him; how he felt isn't for me to answer. I can only speak from my heart and how I felt I was treated. Two different views, neither are wrong. **No one truly knows what you feel but you**.

Toxic Connections: Freeing Your Demons

It took me a while to understand that I may have been toxic in someone else's story and not to be selfish.

I can only validate my feelings. I can respect everyone's feelings are valid. Apart from growing, I learn to see all perspectives on every situation and understand I will not understand everything.

There are always two sides to every story; there's no right or wrong, and both feelings are valid and shouldn't be treated as less. *I dealt with mine*, healing and growing.

Toxic Connections: Freeing Your Demons

      My toxic trait was ghosting loved ones when I should have had open communication, but once words were spoken and lost, I thought setting myself free at any cost was all I had left. Now, I'm holding love in my heart while wondering "what if"....

It's a bittersweet feeling. I did what I thought was best for me while being toxic to them. I didn't see another way through; I only saw the way out. Even though the love still resides here, I'm at a place in my life that wouldn't make sense to them; we grew too much apart.

It's true; we're all toxic to someone; we all hurt someone. How they proclaim us to be toxic. I'm mature enough to take my blame. I know I might not have been thinking about how to spare their feelings. Call me selfish; neither of us was a saint.

I disagree with being someone's every need, and in return, being called toxic because I left. Everything good I brought is suddenly forgotten; all the pain they inflicted has suddenly vanished. I don't believe I'm perfect, trust me, but I knew my intentions.

Toxic Connections: Freeing Your Demons

I won't be deemed toxic to everyone. Some are quick to lie to me, forget they loved me, forget the good, just to paint the picture of them being this saint while I'm the damaged goods. Some may say you can't decide if you were toxic to someone, which is true, but the story is always flawed when the only feelings you're considering are your own.

There are two sides to every story, yours and mine, but the world will have its opinions. The opinions don't compare to what I lived through, so no one can tell me what's best for me or if what I did was wrong.

I know I could have handled some situations better, but one thing I won't apologize for is not giving enough, knowing I gave more than I had to give, just to get buried under your story of me. Jokes on you, your story doesn't define me. I know what I brought to us.

I see everything clearly; back then, I didn't, but now, nothing can make me feel what I did was wrong. I chose what was calling me, what my heart needed. I won't apologize for something I'm not sorry for; just to spare your feelings, if that makes me toxic, look in the mirror.

Toxic Connections: Freeing Your Demons

It's time to own up to your toxic traits and fix that behavior within you, so you don't keep accepting the same in return. It's time to realize it's not always them, but you, too. You're not a bad person because you hold some toxicity, **you're still learning, you're still growing**.

Toxic Connections: Freeing Your Demons

The thing about toxic people is they don't understand they're toxic. When it comes down to who's wrong and who's right, you'll always be wrong; they'll always be right.

Toxic Connections: Freeing Your Demons

The scariest thing I've ever witnessed was someone apologizing for their wrongs, then repeating the same toxic behavior, and having no idea how cold they were. It's scary when you just want to love someone, but *they make it completely impossible*.

Toxic Connections: Freeing Your Demons

Toxic people are so dangerous.
You'll love them,
with all your heart,
without knowing
your heart is breaking because of them.

Toxic Connections: Freeing Your Demons

Opening your eyes and seeing the toxicity in people is heartbreaking. Someone you once loved, and still might, but finding out they're toxic. How incredibly hard it is, *trying to separate the two.*

Toxic Connections: Freeing Your Demons

Toxic people will have you fight for them while putting every blame on you. They will have you chasing a love that was never there, trying to heal them, as you slowly slip away from them. They're dangerous; **open your eyes**.

Toxic Connections: Freeing Your Demons

If you become involved with anyone who takes pride in being toxic, **just run**. *It's not cute or healthy*. You'll end up in a circle of one-sided love and blame yourself for everything that went wrong. **It's not worth your sanity**.

Toxic Connections: Freeing Your Demons

Loving intensely isn't toxic,
it's only toxic when it's unhealthy.

I became toxic when I held the words "I love you" close. You didn't make my heart skip a memorable beat. The love you made me feel was *mediocre* compared to the love I found after you.

When was the moment you realized you became toxic?

_____
_____
_____
_____
_____
_____
_____
_____
_____
_____
_____

I apologized to the old me before accepting my growth. I had to take accountability for the ones I also hurt in the crossfire while outgrowing anyone who couldn't accept the change. I was the toxic one; I've also been consumed by another toxic soul.
My sins were forgiven.

I learned to love from afar. I tried to make them understand how I felt. I tried saving the friendship we built, but it was already broken. I took too much of myself to give to them, just to be painted as the toxic one. That's when I ghosted; I haven't heard a word since; I'm happier.

Have you ever ghosted someone?

Toxic Connections: Freeing Your Demons

Stop allowing toxic people,
Fill you with poison
And calling it **love.**

Toxic Connections: Freeing Your Demons

The saddest part of all is people don't think they have the strength to leave a toxic relationship. Instead of making excuses about why you can't, put that effort into why you should. So many people find reasons to stay rather than reasons to go; *that's where you'll always go wrong*.

Toxic Connections: Freeing Your Demons

I know how hard it can be *to set yourself free of toxic energy*. But I promise you, once you do, it's like a breath of fresh air. **Putting your energy where it's only reciprocated** will have you on cloud nine. Which results in the best decision you can make.

Toxic Connections: Freeing Your Demons

People stay in unhappy relationships forever and somehow find their opinion valid when choosing to find happiness outside the relationship they outgrew. Some just don't understand the genuine concept of love and happiness because *they're blinded by the toxic*.

Toxic Connections: Freeing Your Demons

People are afraid to let go of toxic situations because they hold into every good memory they have of someone and attach to it, thinking the exact feeling will revisit.

Toxic people are like drugs,
Having your search for what's gone
And *destroying you slowly in the process*.

Toxic Connections: Freeing Your Demons

Quit letting the toxic actions of others preoccupy you into believing your heart deserves to be cold after dealing with their unconscious tendencies. That's the thing about toxic people; *they'll fill you up with expectations just to knock you down with disappointments.* **It's not you.**

Toxic Connections: Freeing Your Demons

People fail to realize the toxicity in people and love them anyway. Without realizing there's a reason, you let them go. They'll make sure you're always the root of evil; to them, they can do no wrong. Everyone who loves them after won't get it; to them, **you'll always be the enemy**.

Toxic Connections: Freeing Your Demons

People will showcase you as the bad guy in every story after doing you wrong many times. We live in a world filled with people who sugarcoat who they are for the world, who can't admit to their mistakes; they'd instead blame you.

Set yourself free of their toxic aura.

Toxic Connections: Freeing Your Demons

Not every relationship can be fixed, don't let anyone make you feel like you're wrong for walking away, instead of trying to save the love that's no longer love when it's become toxic. **Some things are meant to be recovered**.

We need to stop the habit of overlooking when people hurt us. Whether it's a family member, a friend, or a lover. If they become toxic to your being, they shouldn't be kept. *Love them from afar*. Go ghost. Don't ever feel ashamed for choosing your sanity over hurting them; *it's okay*.

Toxic friends, lovers, and family.

I don't believe in separating friends, lovers, and family from being toxic. I don't believe in someone being "not too toxic" and others being "too toxic." Toxic is toxic; there's no other way to put it.

I once had a friend I was friends with for years, from high school to adult life, we stayed friends. We were inseparable through high school, but everything before our friendship came from physically being there when it came to our adult lives.

I didn't see this as a big deal if we communicated every day. "How are you" meant a lot. Working two jobs and going to school, the time I had off was for myself; maybe that was selfish of me, I wouldn't know, but I felt like she should have understood.

Maybe that was my toxic trait; I didn't care to be insolated. If I spoke to you every day, I didn't think it was necessary to see you all the time. It was our souls that stayed connected; our lives

were taking different directions. What mattered most to me was keeping her in my life.
I found it draining to fight about not seeing each other if we were always there when it was necessary. The moments that became memorable. To understand our lives are no longer able to be together as often as when we were young, we grew.

It's important to stay strong through the parts of life that challenge you, the parts you're searching for you. Soul-mates breeze through or have been around since day one. Life will always get in the way, but it's your life. Who or what you love shouldn't hurt you; they should love you.

I'm the friend who you won't talk to for weeks, months, or even years, but I can always pick up where we left off. I only fought for soul connections. I always saw the good in them. I was terrified to let go of their memory and not misery.

Letting people stay that I outgrew but loved so much, I couldn't separate the two. I couldn't grasp how you love them just to set them free. I grew up around so much love; even though the hurt, I saw the love. I created love where it wasn't. I expected too much that's on me.

Toxic Connections: Freeing Your Demons

We aren't always meant to love someone through every part of their life.

Being family doesn't allow toxicity. It doesn't give them a pass. It doesn't make them good people. You're not obligated to love your family just because you think you need to. I have friends who are more like family.

Love who shows you they do too.

Let go of who hurts you.

Anyone who drains you of all your love and makes you take from yourself to give to them doesn't deserve any part of you.

What's your lover, friend, or family toxic experience?

_____
_____
_____
_____
_____
_____
_____
_____
_____
_____
_____
_____
_____
_____
_____
_____

Toxic Connections: Freeing Your Demons

There's no difference when it comes to someone being toxic, nor is there an excuse. It doesn't matter whether it's a lover, a friend, or a parent. *There are no different definitions.* **A toxic person is toxic**. All toxic traits are traumatic and hard to recover from.

Toxic Connections: Freeing Your Demons

Toxic people have a way of making you believe you're wrong, and the scariest part is *you become toxic to yourself by believing them*.

Toxic Connections: Freeing Your Demons

PTSD from toxic relationships are a thing.

If only we could all outgrow one another without being toxic to each other. If only we could move on without holding hate in our hearts. If only we could love at the moment and let go when the moment is over. Without feeling broken or wondering **if we're the ones who broke them**.

Toxic Connections: Freeing Your Demons

Just because you love someone doesn't mean **let them slowly kill you**.

Toxic Connections: Freeing Your Demons

People who mistreat you always come back and want you when you're at your best. Shut it down quickly. They didn't deserve you at your lowest, nor *did they love you through it*; **they don't get a second chance**.

One thing I couldn't do was fix someone's insecurities. I couldn't stop them from trying to one-up me with everything I did. I was proclaimed the bad guy. That's when I knew it became toxic when love became tainted and love was no longer enough.

It became toxic,
Our love became tainted,
We became lost.

Toxic Connections: Freeing Your Demons

The thing about me, I won't lie. *If I love you, I love you. I'll love you forever*. The thing you need to understand, just because I love you, that's not a good enough reason to keep you around me if you're toxic. **I can't have that surrounding my aura.**

Toxic Connections: Freeing Your Demons

Toxic people
will always have you believe
you're the one who's dragging them down.

Toxic Connections: Freeing Your Demons

It's essential to make your partner aware of your toxic traits and past mistakes and to not repeat any pattern or behavior. *Take time to discuss your love language.* **Communication is the root of a healthy connection**. To grow in love is to be openly vulnerable, and let yourself feel.

I'm sorry the love we once shared
became toxic to us.

Toxic Connections: Freeing Your Demons

The energy I surrounded myself with is no longer weighing me down. It took me a while to realize how toxic it was and the love I was afraid to leave behind. The memories I never wanted to forget. I was selfish with my heart to people who didn't care to give me the same love back.

Toxic Connections: Freeing Your Demons

I do not love toxic relations. I do not hate on someone's happiness. I'm the one, who loves wholeheartedly, gives everything I must give, and prays it resonates. Prays it's reciprocated. Prays you'll feel it. Chances are,
You wouldn't survive a day being me.

Turning **cold**
Is the most toxic trait
you can hold.

Toxic Connections: Freeing Your Demons

Toxic Connections: Freeing Your Demons

Thank you for giving my work a chance. I pray you chose to get this book to feel what I had to offer from my experience. I know it's not probably precisely what you wish to hear, but it's the truth I've discovered along my journey. It took me some time to withhold this information for it to stick. I don't wish to be in a toxic connection with anyone because the pain stings terribly, but it gives us the strength to walk away. I hope you found that within the reading. I hope you found the beauty in letting go or soon realize it. Come back to this book whenever you need reminders. Highlight. Write notes.

Take care of yourself,
Don't let the toxicity consume you.

Toxic Connections: Freeing Your Demons

Toxic Connections: Freeing Your Demons

Moonsoulchild.com

Tiktok: @bymoonsoulchild
Instagram: @moonsoulchild
Twitter: @moonssoulchild
Facebook: @moonsoulchild
Apple Music/Spotify: Moonsoulchild

Website: Moonsoulchild

Made in the USA
Middletown, DE
24 March 2024